YOUNG
POETS
OF A *New*
ROMANIA
AN ANTHOLOGY

YOUNG POETS OF A *New* ROMANIA

AN ANTHOLOGY

FOREST
BOOKS
London & Boston

Translated by Brenda Walker
with Michaela Celea-Leach
Selected and edited by Ion Stoica
Introduced by Alan Brownjohn

PUBLISHED BY
FOREST BOOKS
20 Forest View, Chingford, London E4 7AY, U.K.
61 Lincoln Road, Wayland, MA 10778, U.S.A.

FIRST PUBLISHED 1991

Printed by BPCC Wheatons Ltd, Exeter
Typeset by Cover to Cover, Cambridge

British Cataloguing-in-Publication Data
A catalogue record for this book
is available from the British Library

ISBN 0 948259 89 2

Library of Congress Catalogue Card No:
90–71088

Contents

Foreword

Romania is a country of poets, poets who not only write but are also published, people who in a world of prose still firmly believe in their art, and their philosophy of essential concepts.

From such a group it is difficult to make a selection for those living under a sky of different words, while at the same time remaining representative. One is inhibited by the vast number of such genuine artists, the inner polychromy of their poetic vision, and the general breadth of the stylistic spectrum. Yet the completion of the task set me by Forest Books, a most important publishing house for Romanian poets, to edit a collection of some twenty of them under the age of forty for Forest's Young Poets in a New Era series, will, I hope, show the poetic vigour of this young verse – a vigour which has continued since Eminescu, and which reveals the perpetual anguish of poetry in this land, as well as the rejoicing. I have chosen representative poems from poets whose names are currently highly respected and in many cases award-winning. But what publisher can ever sleep soundly when he knows of hundreds of other such talented artists who could quite justifiably have come knocking on the volume's door?

The selection of poems can also produce insomnia for an editor. One author included in the volume told me that from his own poems he would have chosen differently. However, it would have been more surprising had he chosen the same ones. In the last analysis, it is always the publisher of such an anthology who has to bear the guilt. Yet I am ready to forgive myself for being, figuratively speaking, a sower. I hope others will do likewise.

Ion Stoica

Introduction

Reading those translations of work by a generation of younger Romanian poets unknown in Britain until now, it is tempting to reflect on the cultural situation in that fascinating country. It is a situation full of relief, perplexity and danger, as any recent visitor will testify.

In November 1990 I was the guest of the President of the Writers' Union in the Transylvanian city of Cluj together with about a dozen members (editors, writers, broadcasters, ethnic Hungarians as well as Romanians). I was scheduled to take up one hour of the time of these busy people, and in the past that would have been my ration, whatever the participants might have hoped about extending the dialogue. During that hour it would have required effort on my part and daring on theirs to get past the courteous and cordial, but rigorously official, exchange prescribed by protocol.

The meeting went on for three hours, extended into radio interviews, and continued in social contacts (very difficult before the revolution) over the next couple of days. My hosts told me that, for them, the immediate euphoria after the end of the Ceausescu years had given way to intense and anxious debate about how literature and publishing could survive in the new free-market conditions. Any sort of state intervention would be distrusted as an attempt by the government to mould the arts to its own purposes. But since the government, beset by alarming economic problems, was not disposed to offer much in the way of subsidy for the arts, that problem was unlikely to arise.

I was also aware, as I spoke, that I was not so much welcomed as a fount of wisdom about Western practices (I had no illusions about that) as an opportunity for these writers to continue the whole debate – passionately – among themselves. Almost every answer I gave produced animated disputes round the table, my interpreter striving to render them to me in feats of simultaneous translation. I could not recall any comparably serious and heated debate in any English literary gathering for a long time; and I felt both privileged and excited to be joining in the new dialogue about the purpose (though sadly also about the *survival*) of literature in post-Ceausescu Romania.

One of the radio interviewers asked which foreign poetries were best known in Britain at present. I replied truthfully – and it surprised me to be giving this answer when there might have seemed to be strong competitors, like the poetry of the USSR or of Spanish America – that Romanian poetry in translation was as well known as any. In the publishing crisis of the late 1970s and 1980s, when translations in particular, always a minority interest among the minority who read any kind of poetry in Britain, had dwindled drastically in number, Romanian poetry had stood its ground. Many informed readers with no special connection with Romania knew about Nichita Stanescu, Ştefan Augustin Doinaş, Marin Sorescu, Mircea Dinescu, Ana Blandiana, Nina Cassian (and other women poets in the *Silent Voices* anthology published by Forest Books in 1986). So how, and why, did they know, and what was the attraction?

They knew because small publishers and their translators had enthusiastically informed them. That had happened because visitors to Romania in the late and most dire Ceausescu years had latched on to a quality of passion and commitment, of poignant and ironical humour, in the work of those Romanian poets they had met and read, something which transcended the stifling official decorum of arranged meetings. Under the conformist surface of Romanian life the arts were alive. The poets, the novelists, directors and actors in the theatre were responding with courage and ingenuity to the deadening and stupid symbolism prompted by the propagandists of the Conductor. And the quality of their work was astounding.

The poets named above represented a generation born in the 1930s and 1940s. The poets now newly translated here had been living under Nicolae Ceausescu for nearly all their adult lives, and now have to decide what differences and challenges have arisen as a result of the events of December 1989. Thus, although they are mostly in their late thirties, they are still a generation in the process of forming a style, and owing less to their immediate predecessors than their first-time English readers might expect. The same images of defiance are there, but the codes are more difficult to decipher, the atmosphere more tense and surreal, with an evident influence of some recent American poetry. There is an undercurrent of affirmation, of belief in the role and necessity of poetry despite everything. But in the statements made by those who have chosen to describe why they write, there is no uniformity of view about the way poetry gets written. There is not yet achievement on the scale of their famous seniors, but there is abundant and varied talent.

Several poets in this selection arrive with accolades from festivals, from magazines, or from the Romanian Writers' Union. It was one of the paradoxes of the *ancien régime* that writers did receive encouragement and prizes, and gather awards, for original and promising work, some of it unconventional by official standards. And the publication of this work (albeit preceded by official questions, pressures and delays) did virtually guarantee impressive sales; every poet here will have sold more copies of books than most of their Western counterparts (though financial returns would have been equally modest). Neither did poets – or others – require to be privileged or 'safe' to achieve these results; the work of the most fawning and talentless of the 'official' writers emphatically did *not* receive awards or command sales.

The fascinating means by which publishers bent or adapted the rules of an apparently inflexible system need to be recorded before the memory of the technique fades. In the entire process the role of the writers' unions (not always the complicit, conformist organisations of Western imagination) was probably crucial. They knew (or well-disposed, discriminating, and above all, strong people in them knew) how to circumvent ideology and obstruction, and open the channel between writer and reader, allowing a communication rarely achieved in the West. And along this channel came work of the kind to be found in the poets represented in this book. The principal concern of the most percipient and responsible publishers in Romania at present is that the free market should not block this channel and corrupt a culture which the former repression failed to destroy.

Most of the work here was written before the extraordinary transformation of December 1989. In the summer of 1991, Romanian writers are still asking why that event has not yet produced poems or novels or plays which successfully catch the exhilaration, the confusion, or (according to your point of view) the disappointment. The conventional answer is that poets, like everyone else, have been too busy *living* life to do much else. The most perceptive books will be written when (some say *if*) things have settled down. The audience will return to the theatre when the memory of the *street* theatre of December 1989 is a more distant one.

The task of these poets will be to grasp, and respond to, a new and different political and literary situation. It will be absorbing to watch how their work develops when the tumult has finally died down and Romania is once again – for better or for worse – a settled society. They have all the skill and resourcefulness (as well as the tenacity acquired under the old system) to ensure an adventurous response to whatever happens next in this most creative and surprising of countries.

Alan Brownjohn

Translator's Notes

Romanian is a Romance language that differs from other Romance languages by preserving a case system and suffixing the definite article. The inflected endings give assonance and chime so that even without rhyme, poetry has an inner music emphasised by the iambic rhythms which are often found in everyday speech. Transforming this music and these rhythms, together with the varied emotions and ideas expressed in this selection of contemporary poets, under the age of forty at the time of the selection, has not been an easy task. This was mainly due to the lack of punctuation and capital letters in many of the poems. In some cases I have been able to communicate directly with the poets but I have also relied on many of my Romanian friends in this country. Together we have shared the puzzle and the joy of discovering this new emerging talent.

First I would like to thank Michaela Celea-Leach for the painstaking and detailed literary translations. A teacher of English in a Comprehensive School in Middlesex, she must have sacrificed much of her precious spare time during the examination period in order to work to my deadline. Then I am indebted to Denisa Cominescu, Lidia Ionescu, Hermine Macovei, Joseph White and Andrea Deletant for giving generously of their time in the final stages. I would also like to thank Ion Stoica, for the long hours involved in reading so many poets in order to choose such a well-balanced, representative selection, and the various Romanian Writers' Unions who helped him in many ways.

Brenda Walker

Ion Stoica

Ion Stoica is a Romanian poet already published in the U.K. by Forest Books. He is also director of the Central University Library in Bucharest partly destroyed in the revolution of December 1989.

Brenda Walker

Brenda Walker is an experienced translator of poetry, and in particular Romanian poetry, having worked with Andrea Deletant on: *An Anthology of Contemporary Romanian Poetry; Let's Talk About the Weather* by Marin Sorescu; *Thirst of the Salt Mountain*, a poetic drama by Marin Sorescu; *Gates of the Moment* by Ion Stoica; *Silent Voices (An Anthology of Contemporary Romanian Women Poets)*; *Call Yourself Alive* by Nina Cassian; and *Exile on a Peppercorn* by Mircea Dinescu. Other recent Romanian translations have included *In Celebration of Mihai Eminescu; As I Came to London One Midsummer's Day . . .* by Ion Stoica; *The Trapped Strawberry* by Petru Cârdu; and *Through the Needle's Eye* by Ion Miloş.

Alan Brownjohn

Alan Brownjohn, poet and critic, was for six years (1982–88) Chairman of the Poetry Society.

Mircea Valeriu Deac

Born in Bucharest, 1960, Mircea Valeriu Deac graduated from the Faculty of Philology, Bucharest, in 1983. Since 1987 he has exhibited mainly in Bucharest, Vienna and Paris. He received a prize for his post-Baroque graphics, rich interpetations of past art and present graffiti, at the Jeunes Artistes, Salle-Bernanos, Paris, in 1991. He has pursued a parallel career in film and literary criticism, and is presently working on a PhD in film studies – Fellini and the Carnivalesque, a post-modernist approach – at the Paris III, Sorbonne Nouvelle.

xvi

Forest Books would like to thank:

The Central and East European Project
and the Soroş Foundation for an Open Society—Romania
for their generous financial support

The Anglo-Romanian Bank for their interest and
encouragement by the purchase of books

The Romanian Ministry of Culture and the Ministry of
Foreign Affairs—Cultural Department for their support in
ensuring that all Romanian libraries and other revelant
institutions in Romania have copies of this book.

Young Romanian Poets
on Poetry

Ion Cristofor

'Above all poetry remains an exercise of freedom, a defiance against all tyrants, all absurd ideologies on which modern man has been crucified.'

Denisa Comanescu

'For me, writing poetry means passing from hate to love. I find it hard to write. And when I've finished a poem which I consider good enough, I feel as if an angel has touched me with his blessed wings.'

Virgil Mihaiu

'If a global effort towards understanding and tolerance does not prevail, then the very 'humanness' of our species will be at stake. I try to give as much joy as possible to as many people as possible. I answer those who question me about politics: my only politics is culture and my only ideology: humanity.'

Elena Ştefoi

'Why do I write? For just the same reason that children play and the dying have one solution – prayer.'

'I never imagined that one day I should start to write poetry. However, I was guided towards such creativity by that earthquake brought on by my father's death in 1971. I was then seventeen. With his death (and he died in my adolescent arms), solitude and questioning, doubt and freedom all found their roots within me.

When I wrote it was as if my father and others who had died continued to exist, while my mother and my brothers grew more real and much more beautiful. Reality became three dimensional. I discovered rebirth not only through poetry in my own language but also in universal poetry.

That was no easy task in a totalitarian regime. My first collection of poems, full of innocence and insurgence, appeared only with great difficulty.

Now, the tectonic plates have still not settled after the insurgence here in December 1989. Yet Freedom again smiles at us, at all of us, in all its naturalness and splendour, just as it happened to my father between the two world wars, when he too was a teenager. From him I learned to love my fellow men, history, metaphysics, dignity, and nobleness of spirit: feelings made noble by the artistic act of creation, day after day, night after night, pain after pain.

Lucian Vasiliu

'I believe that the fundamental reason for poetry is that struggle to preserve thought within the limits of existence, that is within the original and the authentic; it means the struggle for unity between existence and that which calls for it, and possible awaits, it, 'on the other side . . .' Poetry is the embodiment of the meeting between the speech of humans and that 'something else' towards which all our senses propel us.'

Patrel Berceanu

Mariana Marin

'Any poem is a forgetting and is extinguished in the ashes that lit it.

'Why do I choose to write in preference to anything else? For me, poetry is my own way of dying. I write because I cannot really live anything deeply. And while I'm writing I feel absolutely nothing. No thought, no mood moves me. I write as if I have been dead for a long time and am remembering that I existed once before – sometime, somewhere, in a particular place in the universe. When I next return to this earth (to exist means to suffer, and the earth is a place of perpetual suffering), the verses I once wrote will have long since turned to ash.'

Nichita Danilov

'I imagine poetry to be under the sign of Heraclitus – it is like continuous change. So what are they meant to express – this growth, this self-transformation of languge, this unrest of words, all these remnants, verbal, formal (from the colloquial, open and prosaic, to the cipher of metaphors)? Well, I believe it can only be the poet's restless search for 'himself', for poets are those who use words in order to discover themselves. We cast ourselves in many different verbal moulds just to attain that absolute, unchangeable, uniqueness of our being.' This is in fact the essence of our dialogue: few things are as suitable as poetry for understanding and researching the essential and the undefinable. Poetry is the celestial archipelago of our beings. Poetry is a resumé of our lives expressed as light.

Gabriel Chifu

'Poetry can create a moral sense of reality.' *Ion Stratan*

'A bizarre thing happens: sitting down to write, I have the strange sensation that the symbols that make up my own words, the future text, have for a long time already been written on the blank page, and that my role, similar to that of a meticulous archeologist, is, with great care, to peel off that non-transparent matter that covers them, in order to make them visible. The sensation being that I am not the author, but just the bearer of a message between two worlds, to all intents and purposes very different worlds; the go-between of an endless dialogue, which ultimately proves to be – that of the world with itself.' *Marian Odangiu*

'Poetry is like the music of your own soul, a music which can be heard by all but understood by few, a music heard by those who, above all else, possess 'heart'. And poetry is the heart's music.' *Ioan Iacob*

'I am against any statements about my professed belief.' *Mircea Cartarescu*

The
Poems

Aurel Dumitraşcu

Aurel Dumitraşcu was born on 21 November 1955 at Piatra Neamţ and died of leukemia in the autumn of 1990. He studied French and Romanian at the University of Iaşi and in 1976 made his debut in the magazine *Luceafărul*. In 1981 he won a competition for first-time writers held by the publishing house Albatros, but the book *Furtunile Memoriei* (Tempests of Memory) appeared only in 1984, due to ideological reasons. His editorial expertise also won him awards. In 1986 his second volume of poetry *Biblioteca din Nord* (Library in the North) was published by Cartea Românească. He worked as a consultant for the Ministry of Culture in the county of Neamţ and contributed to leading magazines.

Poetry won't keep silent

The poem always resists. First against any form of collectivism, of salvation through the herd. Never in the history of poetry in this space has the poet been more consistently subversive, so that it could well be that all the books of my generation are anti-totalitarian. In an ideological tower of Babel, we cannot come up with a phonic Babel. We would have hoped to hear another kind of 'music'. To be silent means to consent, to fraternize. Each verse, intersecting many other voices and a general state of depression, has assumed a moral sense. To get out of the knot. But how? Every poem – an attempt to gain access to the road to freedom. In all its forms.

Take sleeping pills and shut up

– The sky and the stockings and CIRCE and others entered my house introduced themselves and announced I was one of them. And if I am just so much earth: I'm a handful of earth in which a note-book lies patiently full of rubbish. Because from ink you can make yourself
better clothes
and a passport.
And the sky and the stockings and CIRCE and others talked to me when the dragon walked through that Fayre-of-a-city after blood. I had a beautiful grandmother with wings and she never touched a man but threw herself at the Gods at evening prayer. Perhaps the dragon visited her. How many things a poor woman remembers – during holidays I even grew to understand her, I even dreamed of her!
The sky and the stockings and CIRCE . . .
And everything that's not worth remembering.

The concert

– Some confusing news wants to change the working day of an obedient man. The man stands on the edge of the forest and looks at the town with an ice-floe for a heart. On a sheet of paper his mother prays to a word which just uttered would be enough to cut off her son's right hand or nose so no one will notice him anymore. Confusing news won't fatten the pig in this derelict sty of a life, never and I mean it. I no longer wait for it. I don't much care for obedient men who stand at the edge of the forest contemplating the town. I care for the linen that gives off love from the poorly dressed dead. I care for music. I talk to the owl and converse with galoshes. Everything is black. We're plotting a great concert.

Return of the voice

– No one speaks in verse any more. We've completely tamed
kings, clowns and madmen – everyone
has sent me thanks in obliterated envelopes stamped *porto franco*.
A small sadness came with the first strophes
one could almost say that the page swarms with doweryless maidens.
For many years I've hardly seen myself at fun-fairs, hardly smile in
newspapers – they take the lambs to the guillotine. Those I love. I'm
hiding them lying they're already dead. Alone I've tamed
kings, clowns and madmen, for all of them I've fantastic
news. I wrote this to water: don't mind me, I'm a sad soul
in which geometry is blind yet I'm free.
And what do they think about me, those wild hangmen, when I talk
with their women until dawn? They'll grow silent in the poem, I'll
keep the doors open. But never ask whom I'm reading the poem to while
they're still praying, please don't ask.
The uproar of silence wakes the orphans.

The best year

The year in which you die is the best year. Others have also waited for it, prayed for it wanting to jump the queue ahead of you but you have quietly reached its heart. And you especially wanted a good time with the wife. It is a good year! While she was letting her hair down in vague circles of smoke. You had clothes, good ones, even got into good habits of wearing good clothes – you even had choice – in the town, it rains down over the hubbub of funeral carts. And you've not ventured out again, you smiled together, along with the red wine in the mugs. Then no one added anything. A little blind girl on a wall plays a trumpet.

Yorick from the white page

Poor Yorick sleeps under red rains.
All those from good families have posed
with him. Now that September's here he hurls
in my face: You are guilty! Only you
failed to pose there! I shut myself in the house
I write a word. The word boils over onto the white page.

Dora Pavel

Dora Pavel was born on 29 June 1946 at Sîntandrei village in the Hunedoara district. In 1969 she graduated at the Faculty of Philology at the University of Cluj. At present she is an editor/scriptwriter for the Radio and Television studio at Cluj. Her published volumes to date include *Ante Scriptum* (1984) and *Naraţiuni Intîmplătoare* (Haphazard Stories) (1989), both by Editura, Dacia, Cluj.

The manic mirror

Look for my face in the crankiness of your pirouettes
said the manic mirror and
its senses became – invisibly – disproportionate
seen in profile
Look for my emptiness crinkled wrong side out as far as
the centre of the morning paper
it cried out while reflecting his back
in anticipation
but he, the mime artist, was thinking in vain
of a consoling number
as he gazed at himself devouring
his entire physiognomy
faced with such a perspective
his wrinkled humid palms
would unfold bastard lines
unhalting lines descending flirtatiously
between the fingers to
gradually mummify in an unprecedented
gesture of anxiety

Like death, my love

I think it was only then that we discovered how to choose
when out of everything we chose
the voluptuousness of the most plausible absence
and went off to prune
the roses around the house – except
there were no roses around the house – all we could hear
was their trodden down earth and came out
to watch their eccentric blessing
(as if some forbidden paradoxical coupling)
from behind the fence
but there are no roses even beyond the fence
it was only their trodden down earth – we heard
                    and
at little long last, a little long last (like death) my love
                    and
at a little long last (like death
and its infinitesimal slipping) my love
                    and
at a little long last (like death and its infinitesimal slipping from
counter-creation into vice)

things can be seen so clearly (my love)

Elegy

annoyance at pleasure, experience of a forbidding
landscape –
that old tramp
who lies
with wet shoes crossed upon his chest
no longer begs
(oh! nighttime secrets when our spirit
seeks out amusing remedies of grandeur
by wiping out the texts
forever fresh
with the consciousness of laying out the dead)

Poem

'come with me to the untempting island
sadden me with the blade of grass flattened
by lop-sided shoes.'

but his breath steams straight in his ear
where a remnant of humanity still oscillates
but his eyes squint having no reason
to accommodate

reversed after the intimate inventory a sense of alarm

it's still early
the dolt yawns and satisfied falls back
to the bottom of his glass.

The eye

Tire out my greed! I scream with all my might
and the emaciated hands of my guide
come together
awaiting another guide
what a beautiful way to spend a morning! I continued to yell
a few hours earlier
I'd been shouting
dear God I'd thrown before a world at war with itself
my white eye – that sterile constraint on thought
along with my orange eye – that unfeigned wish
along with my green eye – cruelty's ego
along with my black eye – good taste buried
in a humiliating phrase

(but what if in bright daylight you should again meet that
body which while elongating at one end continuously fills its
mouth with it at the other?)

Nichita Danilov

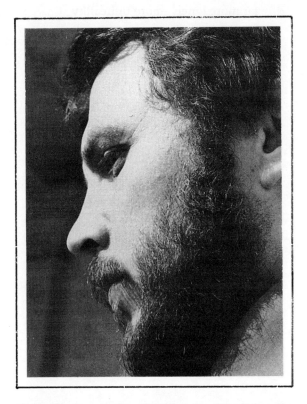

Nichita Danilov was born in 1952 and graduated from the Faculty of Economic Sciences at the University of Iaşi. At present he is the director of the Youth theatre *Luceafărul*, at Iaşi. His volumes are *Fîntîni Carteziene* (Cartesian Wells, Editura Junimea, 1980; *Cîmp Negru* (Black Field, Editura Cartea Românească, 1982); *Arlechini La Margina Cîmpului* (Harlequins at the Edge of the Field, Editura Cartea Românească, 1985); *Poezii* (Poems, Editura Junimea, 1987); and *Deasupra Lucrurilor, Neamtul* (Above Things, Nothingness, Editura Cartea Românească, 1990). The volume *Fîntîni Carteziene* recently won him a Union of Writers' Award.

Ray of lucidity

Like a black leukaemia of stars
my world returns in to itself
far more lonely, more unhealthy

Above, the same desolate images
of your darkened loneliness
and below – black images!

Neither the far away cry of love
nor the nostalgic call of death
disturbs anything inside me now.

And only the unsuffering ray of lucidity
penetrates, colder and colder and without mercy,
any doubt, any hope, any shiver!

Poem of tears

The tear you stamped out with your foot
and the tear you burn with a red hot iron.
The tear that burns in your eye
and the tear that escapes on the waters.

The tear in front of which you kneel,
bare-headed with tears streaming down your face.
. . . You say: there are no tears without eyes
and yet the entire unseen cries . . .

The world's gold

He who sells his country for gold
let him be rewarded with gold!
Let him be given the place of honour at top table
and left there to rejoice.

Let him have set forth the best dishes,
the best wine. Let them bring him
musicians and women, so that he may eat
and drink and rejoice,

and let the people see that he is happy.

Then let them set before him morsels of gold.
Let them press small gold coins in his eyes.
And let him swallow gold by the spoonful
until he swells like a stuffed bladder!

. . . Then on a small heap of gold
leave him to rot.
And write above him in golden letters:
'For gold he sold his country,
and so too was he rewarded!'

Scene with hands and wings

Behind every man
an angel keeps watch. The angel
behind me has fallen
and so whose hands are they,
those fine hands like wings
that so nostalgically
cover my eyes?

Shadow

You'll never see my face
ruffled like water,
you who call me from the depths
and to the depths!

Light mist will form
a question mark
and instead of an answer,
over the lake
a strange flock of swans will spread into the evening,
ruffling both my twilight and the water
but not my face. Because my face is the one thing
you'll never ruffle!

Marta Petreu

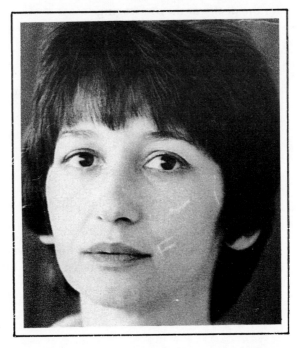

Marta Petreu was born on 14 March 1955 at Jucu, Cluj and graduated from the University of Cluj in 1980. Soon after this until 1990 she was a teacher at the high school, Emil Racoviță, Cluj. During 1990 she worked as an editor for various newspapers and magazines including *România Literară* and *Apostrof*.

She is a member of the Romanian Writers' Union and her first collection of poems *Aduceți Verbele* (Bring Verbs, Editura Cartea Românească, 1981) won her a Union of Writers' prize. Her second book of poetry, also published by Cartea Românească, was *Dimineața Tinerelor Doamne* (The Morning of Young Women, 1983). In progress are a collection of essays *Tez Neterminate* (Unfinished Theses) and a collection of poems *Loc Psihic* (A Psychic Place).

The country's rush towards red

Writers die. Poets die. Of course.

Of course. Now they're just cannon fodder
for the deaf war they're waging
See how their hair glows

We know: they're people like us
made taller by their writing. That head
on their shoulders that mortal uncorrupt brain
I know: that's just like
my father Augustin's brain
yes – they rot
like a library in flames
bodies pulled apart into the earth

And still they come. And still they die. Cannon fodder
they still write   still describe
how earth grows old:
the way galaxies disappear in their flight towards red
On the earth under the earth libraries burn   their nerves
on edge

Still they come. Still they die.

Morning of young women

Uniqueness obsessive singularity
this morning no one is identical to me
when the lives of men
(I loved depending on my loneliness)
become exemplary

I smoke a cigarette
brush my hair like a wig
dismantle that old clock-work of the moment:
could I be equally unhappy
with a man I'd long had my eye on?
with this same cool detachment
would I scratch under the adult-crust
for the child in me?

I list axioms:
No one is identical to me
Self love – negligible

Pathetic and without being demure
experimenting beyond limits:
*psoriasis   acne rosacea   lichen rubra   lupus vulgaris
erythema   exudatum scleroderma*   and certainly
schizophrenia – oozing unlived ailments
the way I never snapped off the real flower   lily of the desert
and even though no one is identical to me
their symptoms come so close . . .

Mask for Marta

You believed – dramatising it – that nobody
needed you any more;
such exercise was futile: one can't get used
to loneliness and pain
A reality without claws   without eyelashes
                                    without devouring jaws
a real reality (and so tautology)
The smiling reposed existence within it
now faces you: you exist for no one
I dust off the festive shoes
but still no identity
I confess; one can't get used to loneliness and pain

A war's forever breaking out between tribes
but never for the beautiful Helen
(I'm just Marta)

Everyday you're on offer like a Christmas tree
like Snow White's red apple
Half your existence rots in the desk drawer
no one writes to it

Heh you! you shout
Heh you! you answer yourself back
Rejoicing under make-up like a prince in a tomb

Heh you! you shout
flapping small wings:
Half your biography like a stuffed peacock
nourishes the twilight moths

The eye that sees

Who can still bear an open mind like a doubtful pregnancy?
The utopia of being happy, happy at any price (What yearning!)
And love, ah *'between one human and another is the most natural*
thing in the world'
wrote Marx
So many sentiments are lost forever
Biography – a history full of blood   world-slaughter

We have no flag for these pains – that I do know

And can one endure such awareness?
With eye-lids closed the eyes see
red veined fountains the high salted cluster
of the nightly rainbow
of the external carotid surgically dissected

in marine cavities through brown algae
dead youth pamper their black feathers:
liberated nerves appear
as if from melted hemp
from the flesh eaten away by the tide

The inferno is just a lucid eye that can see

Oh! who can still bear
step by step
those who
today flay the young dead

Autumn biography

Busy hands: books, vegetables
test papers for Class X11 D
sleeping pills, love-letters, lipstick, vitamins, cigarettes

Nobody waits for me – no one hears my footsteps

Oh. What an unnecessary autumn   what a bloody love
what a mutilated body and such a loss of blood

Blue mould noisily proliferates
The guillotine a childish utopia
compared with the strait-jacket of this gangrene life
compared with the strait-jacket of these tranquillisers
(my stomach rejects them   my brain absorbs them)
Oh! The devious poison of this civilized autumn
the slow deaths

Some boy sends me letters
Each day a frail man systematically tortures me with pity
cuts perfect cubes of flesh from me
draws off precise c.c.'s of blood
squeezes tears from the diurnal gates

What a grotesque biography, women with ludicrous bodies
carrying bags of carrots, treaties of logic, medicines,
used notes, test papers of Class X11 D
manuscripts, the day's make-up, dishes,
chocolate, black grapes, scarves, cigarettes
(Her steps are no longer heard   decay comes slowly)
Some adolescent sends letters
A frail man carves slices from me
What a ludicrous body   what a grotesque biography
my hair turns white like the young dead

Oh God! The guillotine is a childish toy   an innocent
Heinous
I hear the slaughter-houses in my brain
smell my fields of mint
Lashed
my frayed flesh hangs loose

Mircea
Cărtărescu

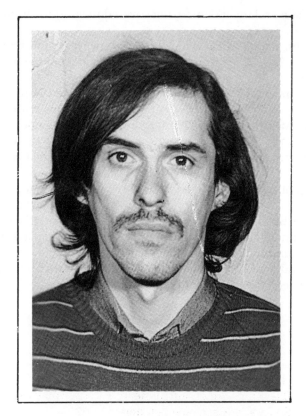

Mircea Cărtărescu was born in Bucharest on 1 June 1956 and graduated from the University of Bucharest faculty of Romanian literature. At present he is assistant lecturer at the same faculty. His work was first published in 1978 in the literary magazine *România Literară*. His volumes are: *Faruri, vitrine, fotografii* (Lighthouses, shop-windows, photographs, 1980); *Aer cu Diamante* (Air with Diamonds, one of the four authors in this collection, 1982); *Poeme de Amor* (Love Poems, 1983); *Desant '83* (Descent '83, 1983); *Totul* (Everything, (1985); *Visul* (The Dream, 1989); *Levantine* (Oriental, 1990).

* * *

casinos and discotheques like some bishop's rings on the fingers of
a bear
the sun and the moon dozing covered in sun-tan lotion, playing 21's
on the lilo
waves, among which is the New Wave, waves emulsifying from lathes,
from body building and from the drill of a seagull.
look how the sea gives birth to all this.
bazaars and bottoms. at the dolphinarium they were splitting the
skulls of dolphins with a dinted chisel
and extracting the small radar. they were plucking out the
phosphorescent screen – the yellow cables, and the blue
swtiches, and clamps . . . at the bowling every medusa was coupling
in the dark hall
bags of castor sugar, the tea-spoon, the instant coffee, a small vodka,
a small lamp at each table
a nice thankyou with a pedigree, a 'it doesn't matter' awarded at Ostia
and finally here I am. you could ask me anything. ask me
if I found by the sea the love that gives birth to everything.
I found a juke box, drinkable beer and a certain Matilda
who took my money and ran off to Venezuela.

* * *

'at a certain moment you reach a sort of impasse, you question it
and it seems to you that there aren't even . . .'
                              any stars
        the car stopped at night in the middle of a field, the others got
out
        we alone were still in the brightly lit cockpit
        the dashboard was strangely silent
I looked at you indirectly, through the mirror
and from the back a green being descended from the stars
made signs to me
because they were stars
a being without a body or a soul
        – what's your name, green being, I asked her
        – my name's Violet, she replied sadly
                just call me Violet.

* * *

seated on a truck wheel the Knight plays chess with death.
over the huge olympic stadium the sun rises up like a tube of Araldite,
                    glueing
the being to its forces, the knight plays chess with death,
then they get bored and start a game of badminton, then they go
                    into the water
then they have a cold drink (a vendor in a crumpled overall forever
                    opening dinted bottle tops
smiling with unmade up lips and from the monstrous badge on her
                    chest)
then they jump in, the knight using the belly flop, and death the roll
the black electronic boards rotate lazily towards the almost empty
                    terraces
the few spectators, mostly students and soldiers, tell jokes about an
                    American, a Russian and a Romanian
it follows the hammer throwing, the body building, under-water hockey,
bowling and towards evening, when the heat becomes more blue,
the knight and death sit down on some cold mosaic steps
and tell each other in a low confessional tone erotic adventures,
                    they divulge their obsessions and foibles
drink excessively and can hardly crawl to their hotel rooms.

* * *

I warn you: in this poem I'll be particularly profound
what I write here won't be understood by many
and some only think they've understood
with each day, each gesture, each breeze, they discover
how wrong they were in connection with this poem
how much they underestimated it, and harmed it with their dull and
                                rigid imagination
with their prepacked and half-frozen intellect; they'll walk
                                through the town
in abject holidays, stained with the smallpox of loneliness
they will go alone to the pool nibbling lemonade and syllabifying
the novel 'War and Peace' when suddenly
this poem will lighten through the pupils of their eyes and Pavlov's
                                dog will salivate abundantly
and they'll howl unbearably on the crowded beach, multi-coloured
crushed by the gravity of its meaning, respectful, hydrodynamics,
                                affable,
this poem is not meant to be understood by everyone . . .

* * *

do you know what this night resembles? it corresponds perfectly
                              with motor parts, a motor
in an engineering museum; do you see how the diamond children are
                              crowding
innocently, transparent, in a crescent space of cylinders and blue gas
lighting their nails; see the trolleybuses carried underground
by blind ants, and the chassis thrown out, empty and polished
                              while the wheels still turn . . .
demonstration motor, a motor looking for its other half, a motor covered
                              with glass, invulnerable, inoffensive,
in which one circle is only in the direction of glinting arrows
a motor in which circulate many cars, driven only by you,
in which the mannequins in shop windows know only you
in which pedestrians allow themselves to be seduced by the arcs of the
                              doors and by your close kneecaps
and by your kneecaps and by your buttocks dressed in jade and
                              sentimental underwear
by all of you, transparent motor in search of your partner
a brilliant set in the year-ring which penetrates the irony of the year.

Denisa
Comanescu

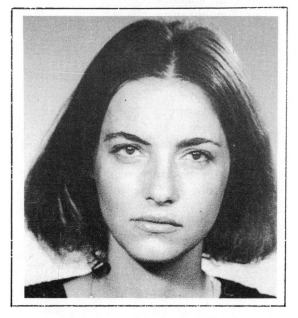

Denisa Comanescu was born on 4 February 1954, in Buzău.
She studied Romanian and English at the University of
Bucharest, graduating in 1977. Since 1978 she has worked as
editor of the English Literary Department of 'Univers' Pub-
lishing House in Bucharest. She made her poetic debut in the
review *România Literară* in 1975. She has published the
following volumes of poetry: *Izgonirea din Paradis* (Banish-
ment from Paradise, 1979) which won the Debut prize of the
Writers' Union; *Cuțitul de Argint* (The Silver Knife, 1983); and
Barca pe Valuri (Boat on the Waves, 1987). She has been
included in several anthologies: *Silent Voices*, an anthology
of contemporary Romanian Women Poets (Forest, 1986); and
Jeunes Poètes Roumains (Editura Eminescu, Bucharest, 1985).
She has also translated from British and American poetry. In
Three Contemporary English Poets (Fleur Adcock, Alan Brown-
john and Jon Silkin) she translated the poems of Alan
Brownjohn (Univers, 1989).

Woman at thirty

While dreaming winged creatures
she oils her body.
Little anaesthetics.
Thought surrounds her
with chimeras
unwilling to leave
the year she commits heresy.

Her move
is a treasure
returned to air.
Oh, Menad,
I should call out to her,
with your glance
the moment comes to life.

But her own eyes
have forgotten
to look at her.

Manifest
in New Orleans

Cut off both hands
instead
replace them by
assembling rings
through which
you are tortured
feelings, moods, sensations
with philosophy, religion,
politics
sex
with ancestors,
with the tongue
So is the Procrustean bed
where American poetry
'insomniazes' itself in the 1990s.

Golden dream

A sedentary cactus stretches
its darkened branches
grey slices of light caress
the typewriter's keys
a few women compete with the paleness
of a small plastic mug
numbed fingers come to life a little
when they lift the official rubber-stamp
                              to the mouth
a silence like a huge clocking-in book
descends into the room
as if we're all being pensioned off
and our names
roll merrily
along the corridors.

Ars amandi

I am looking for Ovid's grave
it is here
in Constanţa
how much nectar
the same amount of poison
an old Greek goblet
adjudicated by Romans
letters to the emperor
little love notes
placed in a bottle
and thrown into a dead sea
Ovid
with his doctorate given
in despair
approved by the Getae
and the Thracians
honor
honour
half a coin from overseas
Under this stone lies
the singer of gentle loves
killed by his own talent.
You who happen to pass by
if you too have loved,
pray
that he lie in peace.
Led by the impulse of 1848
each of us went closer
and each of us prayed
but could not find the emperor
yet mercy has a thousand arms
a station master facing a deserted station
Ovid's grave brings hope
back to us once again
this prehistoric ghost
dreamt-up somewhere
on our shores

Poor destitute country

For every ten pheasants a hare falls
grey feathers like a manger
with a red blade
we peel the fur
from the warm body
a little statue of almandine
fresh flakes settle on the frozen eyes
like a halo

At the Laistrygonians'

I am a fire reddened metal plate
on which time fries fresh fish
devours them
extinguishes the embers
buries me in the sand
until a new orgy.

Lucian Vasiliu

Lucian Vasiliu was born on 8 January 1954 at Puieşti-Birlad, jud. Vaslui, and graduated from the Faculty of Philology at the University of Iaşi in 1981. At present he is the Director of the Museum complex in Iaşi. His published works are *Mona-Monada* (Editura Junimea, 1981); *Despre Felul cum Inaintez* (About the Way I go Forward, Editura Albatros, 1983); a novel *Să Alergăm Impreună* (Let's Run Together, Junimea, 1985); *Fiul Omului* (Son of Man, Cartea Românească, 1986) and *Verile După Conachi* (Summers after Conachi, Junimea, 1990).

January 8th 1954

When I was born, it was minus twenty-four degrees,
the coldest winter since 1944.
Wolves howled in Europe's wounds.
I was bald: father would call me Lenin –
I was like a hamlet
snowed up in Siberia

When I was born
I heralded a year rich in harvest, a year of massive exports.
But mine was a poor soul –
I can remember the old clock
in the house where I lived and thinking about tomorrow's
                                                            weather

Mother was the only woman in the world.
I had no notion of metaphysics,
radioactive dust, the witchcraft of alcohol,
women, suicide . . .

At minus twenty-four degrees, the coldest winter
since 1944

Genuflexion

Harnessed to the body:
clip-clop! clip-clop . . .
I know:
there is no way I can
wrench it from death.
It demands (prosaically)
food
drink
cigarettes
travel
physical exercise.
this very moment
I dedicate to it
five genuflexions
1
  2
    3
      4
       5
and I know:
that not one of these
will ever be recorded
on my death certificate

Mona-monada III*

If you came here tonight
you'd sit in that armchair I bought
from a blind jew –
you'd read to me about unforgettable events,
while my favourite rats
watched eyes filled with doubt
(you incendiary courtesan).
I'd have to convince them:
that you're from the night
where clocks are as liquid
as in a Dali painting

From time to time
I would kiss the abyss of your eyes,
while warning you:
I'm a marathon runner!

My heart:
a candle lighting obscure corners

*The idea of uniqueness; related to the philosophy of Leibnitz

Mona-monada V

She introduced me to everyone:
'a genuine heretic' . . .
She proceeds through the multitudes like a seraph
pointing out my bearded head
which she keeps ecstatically
on a silver tray

Suddenly the lights go out:
we become that first happy couple
from primeval darkness.
We dance murmuring the tune 'Ah, Amsterdam',
I feel the bite of firm breasts.
The snake insinuates itself East of Eden

I navigate
between error and truth
between instinct and rationality
between the dead brother and the live one:
her mouth
is
the mouth of a death too beautiful to describe

Mona-monada VII

Incapable of uttering a single word
while waiting for prenatal signs:
they speak in whispers
about the year which is to come:
I can hear it in the next room
preparing secret luggage

In order to make her a woman,
another night passes,
another tiger
from the tiger's fauna dies

In order to forget
the operations of the spider,
I deliberately shipwreck
in the narrow channel of her breasts.

Ioan
Iacob

Ioan Iacob was born on 29 May 1951 at Ivăneşti, in the county of Vaslui. He graduated from the University of Al. I. Cuza at Iaşi, where he studied Romanian and English. For a time he was a probationary teacher of English and then, after his marriage in 1980 in Bucharest, he had to leave the teaching profession to be near his family. He took what jobs he could find because of the underprivileged position of linguists before the revolution. At present he is a journalist and contributor to some of the best literary reviews in the country. He also works for radio.

He has won many literary awards including the first prize offered by the magazine *Orizont* for the volume *Poemele Luminii* (Poems of Light) in 1982, presented at a Poetry Festival; the prize of the magazine *Steaua* in 1983, presented at the Lucian Blaga Poetry Festival; The Union of Writers' prize in 1985 at the Eminescu Festival at Botoşani; and also in this year, the debut competition of the publishing house *Junimea*. In 1989 came his real debut with the volume *Ochiul Albastru al Nemirei* (The Blue Eye of Nemira).

An ageless man

An ageless man
is never alone.
For whom will my celestial roses
blossom to perfection,
those streets of my massive nights for whom
will the voice wait among tinfoil and stars
if you, woman like a breeze,
won't always navigate, covered by the silver of words
towards an unseen aurora-moment of love

Morning lights up its eyelid

Morning lights up its eyelid,
you wash with cold water, butterflies
of ice
melt in the air,
the green air of fir-trees
receives you – paternal marsupial,
the asphalted road leading anywhere reports to you,
during those first hours,
on the cars lined up – into a beautiful, dangerous necklace.
You yawn, turn on the tap,
the night's last drop of blood.
You'll swallow from the vat of warm milk,
I'll browse through the newspapers.

The road's belly is hydraulically heated – a lizard under the
                                                            sun,
it races towards you elegantly, fast and seductive,
draped in hues of fog,
still beautiful,
chaste Nemira.*

* A mountain near the poet's village, Ivaneşti

I wake in a beautiful clearing

I wake in a beautiful clearing
guarded by angels with blue wings,
transparent wings, blue
too-transparent wings
through which you can see
your childhood.

I wake
in a magnificently beautiful clearing;
the sounds of this epithet
are being defoliated
in a transparent canvas of silk,
wings of transparent angels spread out
in the clearing
as if explaining.

Here I am, lying in the grass of memory,
overgrown by flowers and butterflies,
which slowly transform me
into a book of poetry.

Defying love

Red bunches of leaves
new and enigmatic blood
demanding life
in the arteries

I sense autumn like a fatal love
I am no longer bound to parks
and bye-ways
all roads have a slight scent
of loneliness
austere trees in the watery twilight
lose
all trace
of themselves

loitering autumn rambles
with jacket undone
like the martins
a small boat will come and sever
in half
the lake my life and
the beauty of these words
which out of pity
I shall again
mould
into a poem

Vision through reversed binoculars during the hunting and conversation season

The man with the rifle looks through his binoculars
Everything follows the normal course of events
mothers clean up their babies
grandmothers knit the news

housewives are on autumn shopping sprees
soldiers on their autumn manoeuvres

The man with the rifle looks
leisurely through his binoculars

the tank-crews line up on target
and discover the man with the rifle
smile and open another packet of cigarettes: THE MAN WITH
THE BINOCULARS AND THE RIFLE IS an insignificant point of
reference

They bring a fresh division
and place it on top of the strategic sandwich

the only possible enemy – the man with the hunting rifle

the tanks now seem to be in sufficient numbers
to overcome him

as a sign of protest (not out of fear
of protesting) the man with the rifle peers at the divisions
with his binoculars reversed
everything else follows the normal course of events
(who asked him to go out hunting
during a period of peace talks?)
out of sheer decency the man with the binoculars
stops looking through the lenses
and instead gracefully raises
the rifle to his eye
everything else
follows the normal course of events

Mariana Marin

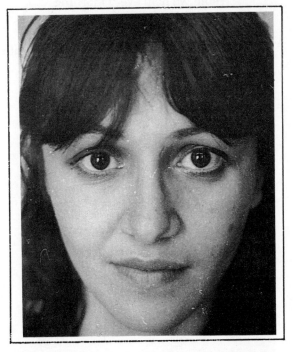

Mariana Marin (the pen-name of Mariana Pintilie) was born in 1956 and studied Philology at the University of Bucharest. Her first collection of poems *Un Război de o Sută de Ani* (A War of One Hundred Years) was published in 1981. Other collections include *Cinci* (Five) in 1983 and *Camera Secreta* (Secret Room) in 1986. In 1990 Cartea Românească published *Atelierele* (Workshops), and her poetry has also been translated into French and published in Paris under the title *Au Carrefour des Grandes Routes Commerciales*. She was one of the demonstrators after the Revolution of 1989 who went on hunger strike, and until recently worked as a journalist with the literary magazine *Contrapunct*. At the moment she is living in Paris, and in December 1990 was a guest at the International festival Points East in Glasgow.

The house of death

All that is left between us
are paper children
whom we help every morning
to cross the road safely.
Refusal to continue the species.
My refusal to be another house of death
in such times.

Destiny

They loved each other
not because they were rarely together
– as was later recorded.
They loved each other because they
                  shared the same fear
and the same cruelty.
They took long walks
            in old parts of the town
and they set up each others' future
                  ashes and dust
                ashes . . .

Elegy II

Do you wring the neck of the poem
when you discover that it creates itself
                              outside you?
A painful revolt and without reason.
Don't be afraid:
there'll always be someone
(a sticky mouth)
to whisper you
the problems of tomorrow
and the history of the past.

Elegy XV

I thought we could be perfect
Oh, holy short-sightedness from my
                                    dimmed eyes
whern it matches your blindness in the
                              face of concrete things!

I thought we could be perfect.

The historical crab

Flower of death, our indifference.
We withdraw from the world with the
                    perseverance of the crab
We allow him to be right
to bury us in the stillness of night
to relish the pleasure of our smell
when inkpots are open
and our words are nailed,
                    flowers of death.

Illuminations

We are getting on better and better
in our empire of dried leaves
and we crown each other in turn
in the four dilapidated chairs
from grandmother's time.
Better the sweat of weakness
than the buzz of power – you say
and the painted buds on the teacup
                                    begin to bloom
(at last this is a perceived necessity
of our sick eyes).
Every morning we also criss-cross
                                    the terrace.
Better the sweat of the noose
than the buzz of power
– I still hear, you still hear
what we have been
what we certainly will be,

necessities finally perceived
by live worms.

Text that looked left
and then right

What about this text
that clots on my hands?

'The Dictator – a friend was
narrating chillingly –
one day following the characters
                        created by a writer
reached a desert
near a deep, deep, deep fountain.
It happened that he came across a
                            wise man
who had a white, white beard . . .
whom he asked:
Haven't you seen these shadows
I've been following since sunrise?
Hasn't your sight been struck
by their devilish skeletons?
Haven't you wanted
to vomit at the smell of their corpses?
Then the wise man looked left
                        and then right
and hid within his own shadow
like a deep text in its own depth.'

What about these hands
that clot around my neck?

Ion
Stratan

Ion Stratan was born on 1 October 1955 at Ploieşti and studied in the Faculty of Philology at the University of Bucharest, graduating in 1981. At present he is the editor of the magazine *Contrapunct* (Counterpoint). He has published three volumes of poetry: *Ieşirea din Apă* (Coming out of the Water, Editura Cartea Românească, 1981); *Cinci Cîntece Pentru Eroii Civilizatori* (Five Songs for Civilizing Heroes, Editura Albatros, 1983), and *Lumina de la Foc* (Light from the Fire, Editura Cartea Românească, 1990). His work has also appeared in the anthology *Aer Cu Diamante* (Air with Diamonds, Editura Litera, 1982).

dawn

The wind makes
cutlasses from corn-cobs
breaks the asylum of inertia
on Japanese vases

a rooster cuts out forgetfulness
your hearing uncovers me

horns flow from snails
and a thousand times more clairvoyant
your hands flow from shoulders
without any pain

happening

they're writing on my hand
'eleven million dead'
they're showing me photographs
of raped teenagers
– please let me go
I've got to get
to the other side of town
they've given me the address
of an orphanage
and the hunger statistics
with eyes closed
– please let me go
I have to catch the bus
it's only ten stops   the bus
I start to shout
knowing I'll be late
very
very late

for a poetic treatise

    – les tendances des eaux du
danube pour les deuz jours suivants –
mother approaches
necessary and believable
– forgive me my job's dangerous
I write poems in the capitals of the world –
the century approaches
(in roman numerals)
      XX
– only the sails are left
the windmills burnt out long ago
in their own way believable and necessary
God approaches believable and necessary
– each of us represents
49 per cent of You – I told him
the rest is silence

now nothing

now nothing
with this existence
above and below this placard

now half
a lung batters the air
gathered by the lower case 'o'

now everything
– snow flakes echo
over the field I've warmed

tightening the lids of night
over towns where once
we made love together

kant orient express

suddenly your heart wipes the windscreen
at eighty moves a minute
suddenly your lungs stir the leaves
a hare crosses the glass like
the needle of an E.C.G. machine
you are listening to the music of the spheres of influence
about the third world and lastly
about the reversibility of life
and the uniqueness of existence
about the revolution of evolution
philogyny repeating ontogeny

is someone signalling you, no it's just the window defrosting
is someone signalling you, no it's only a match struck on the glass
but you try to signal with at least fifty arms
you, eyes with a being out front

Augustin Pop

Augustin Pop was born on the 13 September 1952, in Panticea, Cluj. He studied Romanian and Italian in the Faculty of Philology at the University of Cluj, graduating in 1976. At present he works as a scientific researcher at the Institute of Linguistics and Literary History at Cluj. Between 1978 and 1976 he was editor of the magazine *Echinox* (Equinox). He has two volumes of poetry: *Ceea ce Fulgerul Amîna* (What Lighting Postpones, Editura Dacia, Cluj, 1981) and *Apropierea* (Nearness, Editura Dacia, Cluj, 1990).

He has also published poetry, literary criticism, essays, translations, prose and linguistical studies in various Romanian magazines.

In 1976 he received the poetry prize of the magazine *Amfiteatru* (Amphitheatre) and in 1990 the prize of the magazine *Poesis* (Poetry) for the volume *Aproprierea*. Also in 1990 he became a member of the Romanian Writers' Union.

What and why I write

I'm slightly tanned
dressed in a suit of navy
velvet.
At the previous verse
my girl friend entered
cabbage in hand
wearing a brick-coloured dress
low-cut, no sleeves,
with white lace
over each shoulder.
All these little details
stimulate thought
and, I believe, help the reader
to capture the right nuances.
Actually I was just reading a book
in which Irina Mavrodin tries to explain
the process of creation.
She maintains that *Proust withdraws*
to his famous room
lined with cork
because he is writing his works
and at the same time that *Proust*
is writing his works
because he withdraws
to his cork-lined room.
There's no chance of me withdrawing:
(a) because I'm not ill
and (b) because if I did
I'd be certain to lose my salary.
Yet despite this I do write
I write
because I can't withdraw
and I can't withdraw
because I write.
Obviously this is anti-Proustian:
which however does not change the fact that
my girl friend has just finished cooking
a new recipe.

In fact, Proust himself maintains
that genius consists of
its powers of reflection
and not of the intrinsic quality
of the performance.

The apple and the typewriter

On the first of November
we thought we'd like to go to see
Stars of the Soviet Ballet.
We couldn't get seats
so we bought
two bunches of chrysanthemums:
one purple and one white.
My girl friend
arranged them
in a copper vase:
the purple ones low down
and the white a little higher.
Next to the vase she put an apple
behind it
was the typewriter:
The two main symbols
of sin.
I link the purple chrysanthemums
with the apple:
because love is
the most beautiful sickness
and the white ones
with the typewriter:
because poetry is
the slowest form
of nonexistence.

Obligatory letter

With body humiliated
with nerves stretched
to fluorescence
(the soul doesn't even
get a look in),
I feel obliged to write
a letter to Walt Whitman.
Brave American, I know
you're the most innocent
of poets
and your monumental serenity
has always unnerved me.
And how strange it is
to come across one of your observations,
the truth which for months
has had me wandering through
the labyrinth of a nightmare:
I can endure anything
except my own
diversity.

Freedom of action

Each citizen
is free to undertake
any action.
No action shall ever be taken
without prior approval for that action
from higher authorities.
Each citizen
shall be increasingly involved
in action
so that ultimately
he or she shall achieve
passive action
that is to say be involved in continuous action
whilst doing absolutely nothing.

Re-making the world

Towards the end
when one was all
and all was one
and God
was forever stammering,
a non-extremist guy
came to him and said:
'Oh God, just give me
a weekly magazine,
a radio,
and a T.V. set
and I'll create the world for you
just the way you want it.'

God,
although rather surprised
that so little was required
for such a large undertaking
immediately agreed to give
him what was needed.

The next day, while Eve
watched television,
Cain wrote the editorial
for the magazine,
and Abel tried to find
the right channel for
pop music,
Adam, fully aware
of his actions,
set out
towards Heaven

Mircea Petean

Mircea Petean was born in 1952 at Jucu de Mijloc, Cluj. He studied at the Faculty of Philology at the University of Cluj and graduated in 1976. He taught poetry for a time at a club for students in Borşa, Maramureş but is now an editor at Dacia Publishing House, Cluj.

He made his debut in the magazine *Echinox* (Equinox) in 1975 and has two volumes of poetry: *Un Munte, o Zi* (A Mountain, a Day, Editura Dacia, 1981), and *Cartea de la Jucu Nobil* (A Book from Jucu Nobil, Editura Dacia, 1990).

Crust of the day

I've no idea
– My kisser's already been slashed by cutting phrases –
I've no idea what to do with a metaphor
sent as a gift from a greenhouse-window-of-an-evening
washed by the wind with spindles of rain

I've no idea –
I write elliptical phrases
I check over this year's poems   I transcribe
invented mysteries
the true mysteries

There was a time when I was a delta
now I'm an estuary

of course
you deserve more
we deserve more

To such joys simple prayers
I'm sure I've never asked anyone for
anything

Among cups full of dregs and stubs
devitalized veg greasy glasses and plates
in the shadow of a vase
in which someone once put a rose with a million petals
purple ones
crowded next to each other like people
during a demonstration
I discover the crust of the day

horses of night gallop
off the edge of the table

The blind soldier

they caught the blind soldier they gave him a house at the top of an enclosed mound they brought a woman to him they planted a fir tree and tied a cow to it for him the woman gave him children more children the cow gave him a calf the children gave him other children the calf other calves the blind soldier had every reason to be satisfied one day the blind soldier meets a young man the next day he returns home he doesn't climb the mound the third day he doesn't come home the fourth day the young man slaps him across the face the fifth day the blind soldier returns home but the home is no longer there he can't climb the mound for the mound has worn away the sixth day he surrenders the final day the blind soldier is neither satisfied nor dissatisfied, neither alone nor with others he is no longer the blind soldier . . .

The poet face to face with himself

Only the mountain's solitude
can be compared with my solitude
but – what do you know about mountains
and – what do you know about solitude

and so the playful girls of past times
fill the town's library with smoke
frosted breath and amazing conversation
but – what do you know about girls
and – what do you know about the art of conversation

thus the lyrical offensive of a mountain's bubbles
ended with the winning of the major prize
which consists of some unusable gadget
the prize-giving will be in the hall of Rain House
but – what do you know about the mountain's bubbles
and – what do you know about lyrics

so if the low clouds had moved
with a typical Oltenian nimbleness
I could have trodden the paths of the sun
but – what do you know about clouds
and – what do you know about Oltenians

And so the day comes to an end
the library's closed
the prize-giving's over
loneliness is shared
green foliage is a cat on a roof

the spirit of the mourned Ippolit Ippolitici concludes –
'Before you were not married and were alone.
Now you are married and so are two.'

Cosmic object

(Today in the high plateau zone
where each day they launch some kind of
logged cosmic object
the sun is as strong as in the century of Enlightenment
the wind blows light to medium
there's 39 degrees in the shade)

I'm stuffed with anything you'd find
in the wardrobe of an arsenal
– I reckon as they're fast disappearing
there's a distinct shortage of vulture feathers –
I'm just like a laughable Icarus
or an electrified cross
but lucky to be biologically highly-resistant

the cardinal points are supporting pillars
the sacrificial flames come from earth's core
low-flying swallows swoop in flocks
pattering the tom-tom
their ritual dance repeating the same movements mechanically
could be for triumph or agony.

then the light shatters into fragments
modestly covering everything stripped of a name
the ocean stinks like a rotting corpse
I climb to heaven in a halo of incense
earth is compressed to the size of a bumble bee
swallowed by a thrush – bird of death
the umbilical link to the cosmos severs itself
tumbling I
        fall
        fall
        fall
in a bottomless pit just a roaring
time flies with the speed of light towards absolute O
and the rest – silence.

The wall

the self in us lived
as in the double section of a briefcase

'Why don't you do something about it?'
it heard from accusing voices far away
sometimes it could even see the faces crowding one into
                                                    the other
'we don't understand you'

but he had a yellow sandpaper of a skin
and always had his face to the wall
it was as if some bilious teacher had punished him
only to forget him forever
he felt a hand with black impersonal fingers
creeping up his body –
the breathing of the shadow or perhaps
his own breathing

He divided his existence
with a fish-tailed bird
hazelnut-head
being hunted by a rod baited with a thousand hooks
(I think someone took it for
the famous 'bird of loneliness')

In the beginning he was rarely able to enter the wall
as a mist or damp patch does
later he never left it except
to exchange a book from the shelves
or to burn yet one more thing
killed by its own memory

on the other side of the wall others
gouge out their own eyes or make eyes at each other
in a total delirium of communication.

Ion
Cristofor

Ion Cristofor was born on 22 April 1952 in the village of
Geaca in the county of Cluj. He graduated at the faculty of
Philology at Cluj University in 1976. Between 1973 and 1976
he was an editor at the magazine *Echinox*. Since 1986 he has
been editor at the magazine *Tribuna* in Cluj. He has pub-
lished two volumes of poetry: *In Odăile Fulgerului* (In Rooms
of Lightning, Dacia Publishing House, 1982), and *Cina pe
Mare* (Supper on the Sea, Dacia, 1988).

Like a million hammers on stone

Like a million hammers on stone
the wind beats, resounds in the armour
of a thousand kings.

So, join me at my evening meal
but put aside your blinding iron gloves
and let's talk in the silent language of earth
because I know no other
in the language of the glass of wine
which stays untouched before you.

I greet you silent as the sea at sunset
clean in my poverty
like the trembling flame where the lioness
breast-feeds her cub.
Now I no longer know if anyone still prays
for my humble life
a wasp caught in the honey of the century
but, you see, I don't try to make you give in
with the wisdom of the old masters of the world
with the science of those who before your very eyes
beat down the gates of power or beauty
with the blind man's stick. But please, taste the bread of
                                        my illusion
and like me wear
the sack-cloth of poetry (at least for a season)
drink at this meagre supper from my bitter wine
and listen how the wind of your breath
beats on the body of a thousand kings
like a million hammers on stone.

The mowing of loneliness

Oh, the mowing of loneliness
with golden fruit on stone tables
fruit which no one covets

When you never succeed in climbing all the night steps
without hearing bees climbing from the abyss
busy in the comb of your verse

Listen only to the trees spreading into the wind
the passing over money of the dead
the snails slipping on the sheets of your lovers
on their dresses white as the shark's belly.
Listen to the deep river which flows from your eyes
into the slow constellations born
caring nothing for silence, the syllables
of your poem
written now by a far off
stranger's hand.

Late autumn

Late autumn
shining like instruments of torture
and your brow like sacrificial stones
polished by the hair of victims

The wine of October flows onto the streets
and the sky violet as the eyes of mummies
floods the trees and the buildings
the marble halls of a palace
in which your blood is a red oriental rug
where your subjects step

Ah, far off thunder of some last downpour
resounding like a memory of summer
and the song of sirens who retreat into your smile
the mountains are now crystal
you are pure as the flame
silent as the ash on the altar

soon you'll fall asleep on the water
with the sky pushing against your tongue
quickly cast off the plague-ridden clothes of glory
let it flicker, hop about
like sparrows
on the stained bronze of statues.

Night traveller

Your earth coloured cheeks
with their lines recalling
the sun's writing on endless headstones
and the houses inhabited by the dusty south wind
by a gypsy woman looking after cats
whose mewing opens the locks of night.

The tramp of the barbarians, the tide of cries and shadows
flooding the golden pavilion in which
blind memory walks
through a labyrinth of mirrors.
The wedding chamber of the beast resounds with the song of
the barrel organ
reptiles with phosphorescent blood
leap out from under the phrases of the scribe.

The sun returns to the trees of night
a cathedral on fire floats over waves
moved by your breeze
underground choirs appear from under the threshold
of the house

The lioness near a flame licks her cubs
ignoring the wind which builds on dunes and cliffs
the sand kingdom
of your disquiet.

Happy were the days

The tattooed arm of the sunset places itself
on your shoulder
and a few sleepy stars descend
in our wine glasses
the sea steals lustre from your eyes, from your dress
and the air is suffocated by cricket clocks
and the shrill cry of seagulls.

Somewhere the wind turns the pages of a book
in which the sun was nothing else my darling
but the head of a Babylonian queen
dragged behind a quadriga
driven by bloodthirsty soldiers through desert sands
and the beautiful head of the queen was like your head
my darling.

Happy were the days of the short holiday
the children played on the cliffs with crabs
the shadows of years fell brightly over us
the moon in the sky was a sickle
a golden scythe gliding sleepily.

Elena
Ştefoi

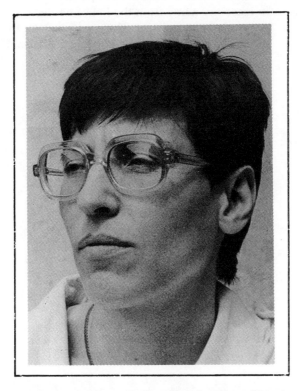

Elena Ştefoi was born on 19 July 1954 in the village of Boroaia in the Suceava district and graduated from the faculty of Philology at the University of Bucharest in 1980. In 1983 she won the Debut prize of the Writers' Union with her poems *Linia de Plutire* (Water Level, Cartea Românească). This was followed in 1986 with *Repetiţie Zilnică* (Daily Rehearsal, Eminescu). In 1989 came the volume *Schiţe şi Povestiri* (Short Stories, Cartea Românească), and in 1990 *Cîteva Amănunte* (A Few Details, Albatros). At present she is editor of *Contrapunct* (Counterpoint), a weekly magazine run by the Writers' Union.

One sunday in May in three scenes

What will death leave me this afternoon:

a war far more beautiful than poetry
to erase my name from the list of heroes.
A sun that can now set. The empty side of the bed
where the mistake suddenly bears a thousand buds.

Even the heart beats

From the outside you can see a Christmas tree. Nothing
opposes us. At this very moment we decide about:
misunderstandings, mistakes, accidents and disasters.
Rose water. Great and simple ideas. Who could believe
the justified hell of this equilibrium?

With the pride of a well-sharpened pencil, the last insomnia
keeps watch so I'm unable to remember what I suffer. But
                                                    between
last year and memory, full of bruises, lies
the description of the facts. I summon courage to ask for help,
see, even the heart beat's had enough of involvement
with the press. Left alone the blood protects
a guilty nightingale. It will receive the punishment of those
who make reality submit, muzzle on paws.
You're young they say and the desert, the desert
passes through the calendar more victorious than any legend.

At the right angle

The tic-tock of the alarm clock knits a noose
between four walls. With so much artistic courage
the earth moves from under your feet – breakfast,
lunch and dinner find you at the right angle.
Well – thanks, even your words have decided to live.
At just the right angle, without passion or reproach.
Oh yes, there are great dangers: the small worms
and good manners have already conquered a street end each,
(I ought to be afraid like my grandfather feared magic,
you say I should be preparing my boots for the enforced
march). Under your pillow a few plump figments
dig a grave whenever you're desperately in need
of silence. And they also take turns to tickle your soles.
You never laugh, never hit out, insomnia is still proud: they bow
before it on market day. I ought to fear –
as my great-grandfather feared the black death (you
wonder if the smell of dead flesh seeps from the papers.)
Poliomyelitis and vain grandeur. Draught and the heroism
of 'would be' criminals, the devil himself more demanding
than the war wounded. That second when you're unable
to begin all over again.

Daily solution

And even now, unprepared,
the miewed confession has no logic:
even as I start to speak,
even as I utter two sounds
inescapable time unfolds, behind and ahead of Time's spindle,
stubble which burns with great flames.
To rise, not even to turn my head
to fall deeper into the imagined greenery,
into the cool of that exile, there from where
one cannot even see the world upside down,
or its suffering? To lose myself
behind a small silky corner
even though my first cry
would fall into the narrow trench
between the two shores of redemption?
How can I rise with this headstone
stuck to my back
where the last smile of my mother
has built a nest?
So judge me, come on, judge me
because my mouth has no desire to
leave the burden and he who carries it
to the mercy of fate and the grinding of teeth, the grinding of
teeth, and certainly not yet,
at least not until the many, too many angered spirits
gush onto the page.

Harder than any of these

Few things are learned through fear. End
of the week and ultimately a monologue with alpine scent
why should you know it by heart that precipice laid on the table
like a mirror in the houses of the lonely, why should you know
it by heart if you still can't make it an abstract.

Through my own free will, I am no longer a sunset.
Knotted wisdom. It's more difficult for the full stop to be
                                          split into
the past, for the languages of mankind to swallow each other,
                                          than it is
for the flesh of your successors who praise doubt. Harder
                                          to stand
on this precipice
and force yourself over it, pulling it conscientiously
at least once
from one side to the other.

Marian
Odangiu

Marian Odangiu was born on the 16 May 1954 in the Turda
district in the county of Cluj. He graduated in Romanian and
Latin at the University of Timişoara. His debut came in 1973
with a group of poems published in the anthology *Virste de
Lumină* (Ages of Light). He also published two volumes of
literary criticism entitled *Romanul Politic* (The Political Novel,
Facla Publishing House, 1984), and *Aternativa Labirintului*
(The Alternative to the Labyrinth, Libertatea Publishing
House, Novisad, Yugolsavia, 1990). He is a member of the
Romanian Writers' Union and at present is literary advisor to
the Writers' Union in Timişoara.

You or about love
(excerpts)

IV

the ballerina has fallen in love with the tram rail
and is watching me moon in stomach
the rails are far longer than the despair of cats
on a tin roof
the shadow of a trumpet slides
into the neighbourhood
a woman succumbs to too much love
what a pity that here
there's no one who knows a thing about writing
no one to stand
between them all

V

Odd things have been happening here for some time
lilacs bloom in January
girls fall in love before birth
John, the poet, has opened a modest bar
and sells plum brandy in pint glasses to soldiers
on the nearby building site
where I was nearly hit
with the arm of a digger
slightly drunk
among the posters of Lenin during the Revolution
pasted
on the walls of this tiny bar
of John the poet
anxious
as after the taste of a strawberry stolen
from between the slats of his masters' fence

VII

then you came and said
man and wife can't be together
unless a deep peace is roaming through their thoughts
(but it appears you weren't talking
about love
I'd started to confuse things)

one cannot love, you added,
by sharing yourself, and dividing into
conquerers and conquered
(the most accomplished form of love accepting freedom of
                                                    your partner)

a leaf sweats out over your words
and holds my gaze:
so you were talking about love after all

only by chance you stated
I'm afraid you believe in bad omens

(you talked about love
and I was imagining your shoulders
the contour of a December night)

IX

I'm afraid it will be hard to recognize you
because of all my friends
only you have the habit of hiding
in my words
and talking to me
about things I never wanted to learn about
for instance
planting a walnut tree in grass soaked by rain which has fallen
                                        from your hair

or to bury myself in its place
up to my breast
leaving you to mix my words
like coloured cards
and to tell me something
about the solitude
of the Knight Christopher Rilke

XII

our love is this clear water
in which we mirror ourselves
taking each other's face

it is the peaceful flow
of its nontransparent ripple
which we guard from both sides

we will never be together
as its banks will never be together
if the river is to remain whole

just like them
forever close
then to be lost
in the gentle infinity
of the sea

Dan
Damaschin

Dan Damaschin is the pen-name of Damaschin Hărdăut who was born on the 10 January 1951 in the village of Prunişor in the county of Arad. In 1974 he graduated in Romanian and Latin at the University of Cluj. As he refused to take up the teaching vacancy offered to him in the countryside he was forced to undertake a string of unqualified, manual jobs in factories, but later worked as a librarian. At present he lectures at the publishing house Dacia in Cluj. During his university years he was a member of the editorial staff of the students' cultural magazine *Echinox*. His debut as a poet was in 1968 in the magazine *Familia*. His editorial debut was in the volume *Intermundii* published by Albatros in 1976. Other published volumes are *Reculegeri* (Recollections, Albatros, 1981); *Trandafirul şi Clepsidra* (The Rose and the Hourglass, Albatros, 1985); and *A Cincea Esenta* (The Fifth Essence, Dacia, 1989). His volume The Rose and the Hourglass won him the Cluj Writers' Union Award.

A pitiful state

Someone's coming to confession who finds it more and more difficult
to meditate;
'More and more, I find it harder to use human speech;
Head in hands, I lock still, taking in the ruin of my own destiny;
I cannot believe that all this debris, those broken pieces before me
were once a block of immaculate marble
From which a gifted hand could have carved the trunk of a miracle;
My dream is a cauldron seething under white heat,
splashing hands and face with tears of tar;
About me people make signals I don't understand; within me
Grows a strength – dark ivy; a struggle begins to ripen;
Thorns of resistance cross the night paths of my blood
Like one trying to master the fury of an oil well ready to blow
Like one ceaselessly fighting floods of tears ready to flow.'

The fifth essence

Inside me is a judge who so far has remained silent
And has no intention of sentencing me until my last breath;
I can sense his tireless watch in his lifelong stillness
Without a sign of acceptance or reproach on his part;
I'd like to speak for him, say it before he does;
I was always guilty of taking words out of the mouth of this Presence
Instead of letting him address me, unveil himself before me,
From now on there's no pact, no rainbow of coming to terms with
myself.
There's only a darkness giving birth to decay, magnets of annihilation
attracting a race
That, dooming itself to eternal wandering, passes on the Secret.
What should have been said has gone forever from my lips
I am just a mountain of recrimination I impose upon myself;
I exist only in what I can prove escapes me, that which avoids me.
Struck down by what's taken from me, my existence is but a sign of
remoteness.

The birth of a poem during the plague

1.

A poem has no power to choose its star sign and hour of birth;
(In vain one summons the unseen between lightning and the tree
                                    chosen for rest)
On the threshold, swept by snow where horror unveils itself,
the poem lies without meaning – like a sentence of death
                        written in someone's blood on the snow
without strength to oppose the gravity force of evil;
without a conductor's baton to assert its power on the dark torrent
                                    of voices;
only darkness taking prisoner the one who came among them to share
                                    the secrets;
only a vast waste which threatens never to leave;
only the taste of resignation forever lingering on your lips.

2.

A hundred winters added together give you the age of the poet-
forced to piece together maps of underground passages showing the
                        exquisite order of rat tunnels;
forced to 'pour news of death into a dead ear',
moaning, like a new Job who has lost
the wealth of blessing, made poor by the loss of grace and visions,
the only thing left to contemplate being the plagued spirit on the
eve of the end of the world,
completely unaware that a bet's been placed on the reason for his
                                    existence,
lacking pride in a certain metal specially chosen for its strength of
                        endurance under the blows of the forge
a poor receptacle for the groans of its surroundings, made ill by the
                        sight of so many illnesses,
a bunch of antennae picking up a continuous wailing, the premonition
                of the furthermost boundaries of the Being

My fellow creature, Heraclitus*
(extracts)

I.

my voice thickens, it grows darker like the blood of a bull
gushing in torrents of tar on the slabs of the abattoir
my soul longs for times when it owed no one anything
a diamond which didn't spare the stained glass of paradise
'the only punishment to reach you is that you bring on yourself'
and
'you blamed yourself better than anyone else could
                                        have done'
voices with as many funnels for the poem to ooze its nightshade
                                        into my ears;
I have forged alliances with the most vunerable and fragile part
                                        of being
and here I am trying hard not to stop this long nightmare but prolong it.
(my tear is aimed to meet an old tear shed a millenium ago)

---

* Heraclitus c 535–475 BC was a Greek philosopher who believed that all
  things imply their opposites, that change is the only reality and that
  permanence is an illusion. He also held that fire was an underlying
  universal substance.

V.

Utterly shameless, like themselves, that's how the gods think of you
capable of divulging the illness that they all avoid naming;
when underneath the petrified lava you are only a sob eternally

postponed;
You feel like running   like deserting from that privilege with which
they tempted you
far away   from the devastating poem that leaves your lungs
without one drop of air,
to shelter your body   an open wound   in a salt mine;
If you laid your confession before the jackal's burrow,
you would think your soul completely weightless.
(compared to your tear, Heraclitus, all cause for crying seems

unimportant).

Gabriel Chifu

Gabriel Chifu was born on 22 March 1954 in Calafat, a little harbour town by the Danube. He graduated from the Nicolae Bălcescu High school in Craiova, having specialized in Mathematics. He then attended the Faculty of Automation and Computing at the University of Craiova. From 1985 he has been the editor of the magazine *Ramuri* (Branches) and is secretary of the Writers' Union in Craiova. He has received several literary awards and his poems have been translated into French, Serbo-Croatian, Italian and German for publication in poetry magazines and anthologies. He has five publications of poetry: *Sălaş în Inimă* (A Place in the Heart, Eminescu, 1976) for which he received the Writers' Union Prize; *Realul Eruptiv* (Eruptive Reality, Eminescu, 1979); *O Interpretare a Purgatoriului* (An Interpretation of Purgatory, Eminescu, 1982); *Lamura* (The Choicest, Eminescu, 1983); *Omul Neţărmurit* (Man Without Boundaries, Scrisul Românesc, 1987); and two novels: *Unde se Odihnesc Vulturii* (Where Vultures Rest, Eminescu 1987), and *Valul şi Stînca* (The Wave and the Rock, Scrisul Românesc, 1989).

House on the waves

Now I'm living in a country
not drawn on any map;
I live on the edge of a knife,
I live in a house raised up by the waves.

Ah, yes, the time has arrived,
I live on a knife's edge
and the space is enough for me,
it's a large field to me.

Ah, yes, now I have such a fine view
I can see the painful narrowness of the
         edge
a patch far too large
for my heart and mind clothed today
in the spotless clothes of a hermit.

Ah, yes, from my old sight there sprung
another kind of sight, unfathomable,
as a pure flame springs from ashes.
And my house on the waves
stays steady, fixed
and the knife's edge is enough for my
         existence.

Now I look without fear at the negative
         star
which darkens and freezes us.
I look without fear, I look
until its black ray, defeated, whitens.

Café

A coffee, an orange juice drunk at the café in the town centre,
drowned in articulation. What can one do
when that ounce of inner gold bestowed upon us
is wasted, infinitesimally, daily, in vain? I wait
for the day when we'll grow
white wings. That day
somewhere, far away, when some dead embers
will burn again
because of us. But alas, no:
our arms and maybe even our hearts
have turned to gypsum. We are just scribes
who, all our lives have notched but one perfect
verse: our own death.

Nowhere, never

I am on a ship made of rotting wood
which has no water beneath it.
Without waves, without wind for sails,
I still travel:
Silently rocking, the sad ship moves slowly on
towards the unseen harbour.
On what kind of sea is this sick ship floating?

I don't know. I don't know.
And what sort of breeze steers it unerringly on its way?
I don't know. I don't know.
And what's the name of this unseen harbour the unafraid,
                                          wounded
ashen-ship, ship of words, approaches?
Nowhere, never is the shining name of the harbour,
Nowhere, never
Nowhere, never I murmur and my eyes notice
a tear welling up, a gigantic one
flooding the world just as light floods into a summer morning.

Europe under the scissors

It was with scissors that Europe was cut in two.
a crane found he'd left a wing on the other side.
A house had walls on one bank, a roof on the other.
A flower found its perfume on both sides.
One person had been separated from
sight, voice and heart
which just happened to fall on the other side of the blade.
It was the way the scissors lay, oh geometry of scissors.
Oh justice of scissors, may the will of the scissors be done.

Time wept obliged to pass at different rates
over the same soil. (Imagine me advancing with left arm
moving faster or slower than my right). The great night wept,
                                    bearer of peace,
bleeding with a body severed in half.
And the clear day did likewise.
Light itself
sat on one bank afraid, cut off:
How to pass over the precipice, over this dark
parenthesis, how to reach
that other border? Oh, justice of scissors,

scissors that advanced serenely over mountains and valleys,
                    over waters and across thought.

Patrel
Berceanu

Patrel Berceanu was born in 1952. Between 1971 and 1974 he worked in an ammunition factory and later as a post-office employee. Having completed his military service, in 1980 he became a drama student in Bucharest and at present is the director of the National Theatre in Craiova. He has published four books of poetry: *Sentimentul Baricadei* (The Feeling of the Barricade), Scrisul Românesc, 1976) and *Poeme ín Mărime Natursală* (Life-size Poems, Scrisul Românesc, 1983); *Întímplarea cea Mare* (The Big Happening, Eminescu, 1984); and *Lacrimi Civile* (Civilian Tears, Scrisul Românesc, 1991).

Poem

I wrote a poem in blood.
With blood I laid it on paper.
With real blood. Warm. Red.
Those who don't raise edifices with their blood
shouldn't read it.
Those who aren't reaping wheat with sickles
of blood shouldn't read it.
Loud-mouthed politicians who forever waste
the blood of others – certainly shouldn't read it.
Don't smile. I wrote a poem in blood.
It'll find readers, at least I'm hoping so.
Sorrow has settled over everything now.

Our reality

If the world carries on like this
those still unborn would do well to
                              meditate
a little before entering this world
eager for action
Already scientists maintain the foetus
                              dreams
the same images as the mother
so those unborn are already among us
if the dream is just tricked reality
Our reality since we know no other.

My blood and the star's

autumn. the blood ripples slightly, mourning.
i don't know, i shall never know
which window they dreamed from
those women of blue flesh

time has left together with the spices,
behind it comes the cold to nail
the palms of the star.

and how to sing to those women
of blue flesh i shall never know
my blood and that of the star
gush longings down your body   window

The shortest Platonic dialogue

PLATO: You, poet, Amphilos, are renowed
for not praising the Gods or their deeds.
Is it true?

AMPHILOS: Yes, Plato, it's true.

PLATO: Then, oh bold one, what do your verses praise?

AMPHILOS: I praise things, oh Plato. I sing of night and the
laurel, of dew and coriander. Of stone and
waves.

PLATO: And do you really think, Amphilos, that night
and dew, shore and wave, cannot sing without
help? Listen more intently, and you'll hear their
song.

AMPHILOS: You could be right, wise grandson of King
Codrus. But are you not aware that things such
as these are the Gods of poetry. The Gods
themselves are dumb.

Descendency

I would like to be able to teach my son
the difference between a good man
and an evil one.
Yet how? My father couldn't
open my eyes to such things,
otherwise today I'd be ruler of the world.
My father was a good man
so was my grandfather, and my grandfather's father.
I am from a dynasty of Good People
yet not one could show me
the difference between good people and bad ones.
Does that mean that the good fail to recognize the bad?
It's possible.
However, the problem still remains
and my son waits for enlightenment,
a finger pointed: that is an evil man!
For the moment just that.
But of course it's not possible.
And later, it'll be even less possible.

Virgil Mihaiu

Virgil Mihaiu was born 28 June 1951 at Cluj-Napoca. He graduated from the Faculty of Philology at Cluj University in 1974 having studied English, German, Spanish and Portuguese. From 1971 to 1983 he was on the editorial staff of the cultural magazine *Echinox*. Following this he was one of the editors of the International Jazz Federation's magazine, *Jazz Forum*, published in Warsaw. Since 1990 he has been on the editorial staff of the cultural magazines, *Steaua* and *Criterion*. A member of the Writers' Union, he has had four volumes of poetry published, his debut being with the publishing house Dacia in 1977 when he received a prize for *Legea Conservării Adolescenţei* (Law for the Conservation of Adolescence). His other volumes are: *Sighişoara, Suedia şi alte Stări de Spirit* (Sighişoara, Sweden and other States of Mind, Albatros, 1980); *Indicaţiuni Pentru Balerina din Respiraţie* (Directions for the Ballerina inside Breath, Eminescu, 1981); and *Poeme* (Poems, Dacia, 1986).

Five shop windows

And now I shall present
the movements of women – an inventory
up-to-date and as it appears frozen
'on the iced-over windows
of the text

1. leaves in the morning (another frosty word)
for the station
with her doctor's bag under her arm
and walks over hills
and walks over country paths
until evening
once back home
continues the unending war
with her parents
knits – then reads yet again
her general practitioner's papers
lights of the lecture hall now barely flicker
at the edge of memory
the shell brought from the seaside
has lost its echo
and seems an inanimate hulk of salt
the telephone intervenes
and then for a moment the thought of death
vanishes

2. wakes up early
smokes the first cigarette
has a hurried breakfast
is late for work
the boss punishes her
but she grows wet with pleasure
imagining that punishment
her lover will give her
knits
gossips with colleagues
perhaps watches a video
smokes

dressmakes from patterns and amongst all this
plans for the future and amongst all this
tears

3. always running around
raises her child
house-keeps for herself
takes medicine
never smokes – goes to bed early
cooks well
good with her hands can repair things
although caresses still prove a problem
they're in too much of a hurry
to catch life as it passes
being hard-working doesn't
always bring happiness
but the woman can't stop the fire
she's lived in since she was born

4. in the morning
her legs look even longer
storks take off from their great length
melancholy gliding
a mountain of strawberries condenses on her lips
then only half-awake
with her sleepy face about to reach an orgasm
she mixes together milk, sugar and cocoa
in a cup on the small table
the apartment is small as a cell
the furniture ready to fall apart
nothing fits any more
clothes shrink until they're only rags
instead her fingers grow, grow
till large enough to swallow great quantities of rings,
if the Inca empire hadn't already collapsed
in a jungle of times
in a jungle of histories

over ferns and nettles – falling on her back
beneath the mosquitoes thirsting for blood
under the spurs of her predestined lover –
she dreams that no one will know them
except the sky

5. seems to be writing with the cigarette
only reads the pages snowed under the nicotine
does she ever eat?
maybe she only becomes truly devouring
when she melts her lips on my mouth
otherwise
she sleeps on a synthetic couch
without even imagining
the Sun-King had lent me
his great four-poster nuptial bed
to steal her away from smokey images
and lead her to something firmer
straight to the barre de ballet
let's see if she'll let herself be lured
to an improvised show that's truly shared

The ray

the shop assistant gets confused
between the petrol coupons
and the sugar ones
asks for my identity card
shows me where to sign
says: 'Autograph it here with your
                    signature, poet'
the February cold falls vanquished by
the cross-fire of our glances.

Ballet

Their bodies
Become art
For life
Life for
Art
Youth without death
Life towards
Eternity
Their bodies
Themselves
Approach the altar for self-sacrifice
Given
To the winds
Of the four horizons
At the cross-roads
Of the four
Elements
Exuberant bodies
Forgetting themselves
Flying beyond their limits
And over
The given
Limits
Over all
Imposed limits

Attenuating circumstances

sometimes an exercise book's left
a rib
shrapnel

a sketch of your great utopia

while
the barrel of a gun
chillingly licks
your neck
and hisses in your ear
the command to be happy

Traian
Coşovei

Traian T. Coşovei was born on 28 November 1954 in Bucharest. He studied Philology at the University of Bucharest, and published his first volume in 1979. This was *Ninsoarea Electrica* (Electric Showing, Cartea Românească) for which he won the Writers' Union Debut prize. He has also published *1, 2, 3 Sau* (1, 2, 3 Or, Albatros, 1980); *Cruciada Interupta* (Interrupted Crusade, Cartea Românească, 1982); *Inşteaptareă Cometei* (Waiting for the Comet, Cartea Românească, 1986). He contributed to the collected anthology *Aer cu diamante* (Air with Diamonds) and in 1991 published a book of literary criticism *Tornini de la Uni Vers* (Starting from a Verse, Eminescu). At present he is editor of the magazine *Contemporanul* (The Contemporary).

Hunting gun

One fine day I'll climb up the steps to the loft where the rag
                                          dolls are.
In white hospital coat, and in slippers I've had since the time
                                       of the reform,
I'll open the chest where my father once kept his hunting gun.
Wrapped in cobwebs, buried
under a golden cloud of dust
with a blind lantern I'll search for the couch where it rested,
I'll light up the place where it lay wrapped in cloths
its thin metal burning.

Through its barrel I shall spy the world and know how
                                   dinosaurs vanished,
through the sleeves of my white coat I shall peer at the sky,
ponder on the fate of whales, of Hemingway, on the noise of
                                 those still alive below.
Stepping over memory in my warm slippers
all alone I'll talk in the past tense.

But that thin and warm trickle will float amongst us,
follow us day and night, drive us through savannahs and
                                 steppes –
chase us on through unending forests.
One day I'll climb to the loft full of ragdolls and rotting trunks.
I'll climb the steps with great strength, with great strength
                               break the rusty padlock,
I'll smash open the skylights –
I'll rummage for my father's old hunting gun.

For days on end I shall stay motionless, cheek
pressed against its transparent, burning metal.
For days on end I shall descend among the living
hands covered in blood.

Man with the suitcase

There's not much I can say about the man with the suitcase.
By the light of the stairs he has the eyes of St. Augustin.
In the dark they're the eyes of Donald Duck.
Together we shared the same neighbourhood of gaiety –
                             then when it all ended
cried together in the tram terminus at the end of the line.
Without knowing one another
we listened to the sound of butterflies battering the window
                                  of the waiting-room.
Without so much as a hello, we warmed our hands
around the tea of November nights.

A man with a suitcase full of used bicycle parts
in the most beautiful of worlds.
      And so it was meant to be.
      And so it was meant to be.

Both of us equally determined before the ticket hut.
Both of us standing our ground before the filing cabinets.
      Pitié pour les forts!
      Pitié pour les forts! We shouted in unison!
Neither of us saw the sun rise over the pyramids.
Neither of us looked at the Seine carrying the drowned
                                    downstream.

The landlady can talk all she likes.
The man in the corner can shrug his shoulders.
The paralytic on the stairs can do nothing.
Both of us have paid our debt in full,
                 both of us exaggerated about happiness.
He with his cardboard suitcase, descending the stairs –
me, hunting for something sharp to wait for him at the exit.
Pitié pour les forts!
Pitié pour les forts, we shouted at the same time.
I suppose in the end it had to come to this.

The poem

The time has come for me to gather up my loneliness
                                   like a small sum of money.
The time has come for me to finish my poem.
The shouting's over, the heavy rain's about to stop.
Far away over glass oceans
the waterfall of your knees breaks over rocks.

And now it's time for me to finish this poem –
so that I can live
I must close it up like an old military tunic,
I shall close the door, write on walls in lamb's blood,
paint thick white-wash lines on fences,
oil my body in bear's fat
and stutter badly.

Now, I've only got to nail up the window –
turn on the taps in the house, and switch off the light!
    It has to appear, it must be close by.
    I'll cut my hair short, I'll hunt it mercilessly.
Mercilessly snatch the handbag from the old lady in the
                                   basement,
rifle through her darkness smelling of lavender,
trample over those letters from the front,
                               the insurance policies!

It must be here somewhere!
I'll search in the medicine chest, cut out
the photograph with scissors –
with the scissors cut my way through the crowds,
with the old lady's scissors cut out for myself
                            a house, a lover, a dream.

But it is near, I can sense it. For the fur of this poem
I'm ready to let go my friends, to sell my soul,
to slowly paint my face with the ashes of the great libraries of
                                     the world!

The time has come, at last, to finish my poem.
Now, right now (just a little longer, please –
                              a moment more, I implore you)
with this poem I shall earn my life.
It's been here, it's maybe even gone past . . .

Just let me begin it.
Just let me end it.

Future past

Last autumn the band's pavilion was burned,
just today the barracks over the road were 'raised';
I am stretching in front of the mirror more tired now after
                                        so many events.
Tea is served in even thinner cups –
my blue veins visible through their enamel,
veins pulsating to the rhythm of crying and the gritting of
                                        teeth.

So, the wine's finished, the cigarettes are nearly finished,
                                pigeons are getting rare.
It wasn't me who dirtied the blind child's clothes with
                                        boot-black.
It wasn't my feet that kicked in the old lady's door in the
                        basement, I only nicked her unopened letters.
And for a whole winter fed them to the blackbirds in the park,
they sent snow over the town
a whole winter and another winter.

With the paraffin lamp I've burned the pictures of my lover,
with their tender ashes I've smeared my face
so you can see how evil I can be –
so you can see I leave no prints or spots of blood on things.

With a bear's claws night scratches on windows
but I wait for my German lesson and my tea.
With a cat's soft paws morning steps over roof-tops
but I am an old man who still waits for his tea.
With a mole's huge paws
my life will dig tunnels toward you.
But long ago you stopped waiting for tea.
But long ago I ceased to exist.

The silence

The thousand doors have closed–
Behind them an iron silence has fallen over everything.
The thousand windows have been switched off –
in their empty sockets a heavy silence has opened its eyes
                                    and looked deeply into mine.

A thousand doors have closed, a thousand windows
                                    switched off.
On the table, the paper grows slowly black – on the page
                        which grows greyer and greyer,
the whole silence is written in lower case from beginning
                                    to end.
My red hand is slowly sinking into its speechless ashes.

Unwritten remains the cheek pressed against the window,
unspoken – the pain –
unwritten the eyes, unspoken the body far away in mirrors.
A thousand eyes closed – behind them in the silence a
                                    thousand eyes sparkle.
My white hand is slowly sinking in their speechless ashes
which the wind scatters through the room.

Unwritten, the words have smouldered all night long,
Unwritten, near morning, my blood
sang out three times.

Romanian Writers
Published by Forest Books

AN ANTHOLOGY OF
CONTEMPORARY ROMANIAN POETRY

Translated by Andrea Deletant
and Brenda Walker

A selection of work by poets, including world-famous writers such as Marin Sorescu and Nina Cassian, writing under the difficult conditions of the Ceausescu dictatorship.

ISBN 0 950948 74 8   112 pages/£6.95

PIED POETS
CONTEMPORARY VERSE OF THE
TRANSYLVANIAN & DANUBE GERMANS
OF ROMANIA

Selected and Translated by Robert Elsie

Poetry by the German minority living in Romania, many of whom fled the Ceausescu regime.

ISBN 0 948259 77 9   208 pages/£8.95

VLAD DRACULA
THE IMPALER

A play by
Marin Sorescu

Translated by Dennis Deletant

This play by Marin Sorescu shows a ravaged land – a world full of whispers and spies; injustice and despair, where suspicion is rife. Is its ruler a martyr or a madman?

ISBN 0 948259 98 1   112 pages/£7.95

The Thirst of
The Salt Mountain

A trilogy of plays by
Marin Sorescu

Translated by Andrea Deletant and Brenda Walker

Marin Sorescu, one of Romania's most controversial poets and playwrights, has both the philosophic depth of Beckett and his own very special vision about the impossibility of communication in everyday life. Beckett's god is dead, Sorescu's only tired.

ISBN 0 9509487 5 6   124 pages/£6.95

Call Yourself Alive?

The Love Poems
of Nina Cassian

Translated by Andrea Deletant & Brenda Walker

This selection concentrates on the love poetry of writer and composer Nina Cassian. Love is interpreted in its widest sense: not only sexual passion, but love of life, of freedom, and, in the splendidly sensuous final poem, of her own language.

ISBN 0 948259 38 8   96 pages/£6.95

Silent Voices

An Anthology of Contemporary
Romanian Women Poets

Visual details remind us that these poems were written in Romania; but the more intimate and inwardly-focussed areas of the poetry make it clear that these fourteen women have insights and experiences to share with women everywhere.

ISBN 0 948259 03 5   176 pages/£8.95

Let's Talk About The Weather

Poems by
Marin Sorescu

'Sorescu has created a new style in Romanian poetry . . . his rich vein of irony and humour brought him immediate success with the critics and the public . . . The verse written by Sorescu is largely anecdotal in character. A direct approach, exemplified by his epigrammatic caricatures of love and death, distinguishes his work from the oblique, ornate and cerebral poetry of his contemporaries.'
(Times Literary Supplement)

ISBN 0 9509487 8 0   96 pages/£6.95

Exile on a Peppercorn

The Poetry of
Mircea Dinescu

Mircea Dinescu, the angry young man of contemporary Romanian poetry, has already won acclaim outside his native land through translation of his verse in France, Italy, West Germany and the USSR. He appears here for the first time in English translation showing that the problems of contemporary society have no frontiers . . .

ISBN 0 948259 00 0   96 pages/£7.95

Gates of the Moment

by Ion Stoica

Ion Stoica is a well known and respected Romanian writer and broadcaster. His work is a good example of contemporary Romanian poetry where old and new influences are in evidence.

ISBN 0 9509487 0 5   128 pages/£6.95

As I Came to London
One Midsummer's Day

Poems by
Ion Stoica

Ion Stoica's first book to be translated into English was *Gates of the Moment* in 1984. This smaller collection was inspired by a visit to the U.K. and surprises the reader with its original and imaginative responses to places like Trafalgar Square, Stonehenge and Hadrian's Wall. Although the book was printed in 1989, it was not possible to release it in the U.K. before the Revolution because of the ruling that all poems translated abroad must first have been published in Romania.

ISBN 0 948259 63 9   32 pages/£3.95

Youth Without Youth
& Other Novellas

by Mircea Eliade

Mircea Eliade was a great historian of religions but he is also renowned for his fantastic prose. He spins tales like Borges with roots deep in Hoffman and the German romantics.

ISBN 0 948259 74 4   304 pages/£12.95

In Celebration of
Mihai Eminescu

Poems by
Mihai Eminescu

Mihai Eminescu, 1850–1899, was considered a poetic genius, and after his short and tragic life he became known in literary circles as the last of the Romantics.

ISBN 0 948259 62 0   128 pages/£15 cloth